The key to unlocking the power of the forest is in the five s...
Let n...
ear...
fe...
a...
lea...
diffe...
the s... ...ering through the branches. Smell the fragrance of the forest and breathe in the natural aromatherapy of phytoncides. Taste the freshness of the air as you take deep breaths. Place your hands on the trunk of a tree. Dip your fingers or toes in a stream. Lie on the ground. Drink in the flavor of the forest and release your sense of joy and calm. This is your sixth sense, a state of mind. Now you have connected with nature. You have crossed the bridge to happiness.

Dr. Qing Li - 'Shinrin-Yoku'

What is Silvotherapy?

'Silva' is a Latin word meaning 'wood' or 'forest' and so the term 'Silvotherapy' is used to describe a practice that uses trees, woodland and forests to increase mental and physical health and wellbeing.

Silvotherapy is a nature-mindfulness practice that has been shown to:
- Reduce stress, anxiety and depression, and improve mental wellbeing
- Increase the body's immune response
- Improve creativity, concentration and reduce mental fatigue

Silvotherapy Invitations

'Invitations' are activities designed to encourage you to connect with the natural world around you through your different senses. They can heighten your sensory awareness and enhance the benefits of increased nature connection.

A Small Book of Silvotherapy

by Hugh Asher

Is it like Shinrin-Yoku or Forest Bathing?

Shinrin-Yoku is a practice with its origins in Japan, that translates into English as 'Forest Bathing'. Forest Bathing usually involves walking slowly and leisurely through the woods or forest, immersing yourself in the natural environment and mindfully using all of your senses.

Silvotherapy is very similar to Forest Bathing or Shinrin-Yoku in that they both involve mindfully connecting with nature. But whilst Forest Bathing walks are often 2 to 3 hours in length, Silvotherapy sessions are usually shorter - about 20 to 40 minutes in duration - and often have a greater focus on the sensations associated with touch and proximity to the trees than Forest Bathing.

In the same way as Shinrin-Yoku, Silvotherapy is all about accepting the forest's invitation to slow down your thoughts and steps to the pace and rhythm of nature.

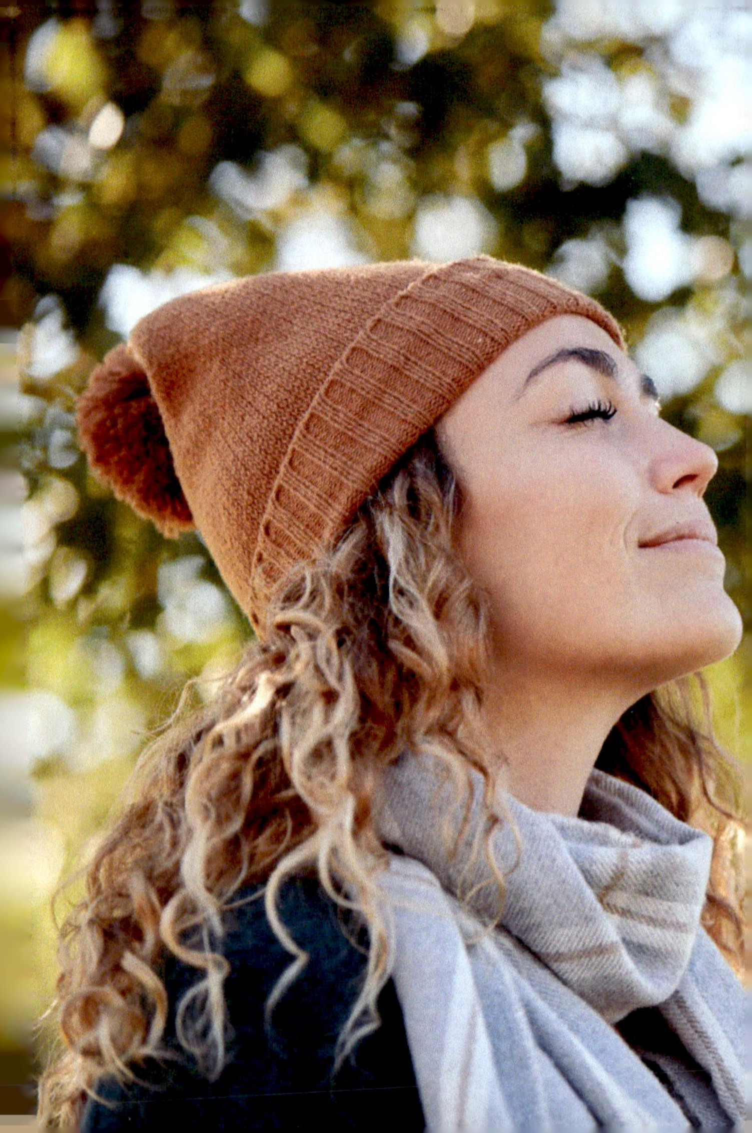

Finding the Pause

It often helps to start your session of nature-connection activities by focusing for a little while on your breathing.

Take a long, deep breath, in through your nose, and then out through your mouth. Notice the quiet moment between the in-breath and the out-breath, the pause.

Repeat this cycle of breathing 6 to 8 times, focusing on the pause between each inhalation and exhalation.

'Finding the Pause' can help to clear your mind, calm your autonomic nervous system,* and help you to connect with how you're feeling now, in the present moment.

* Your autonomic nervous system (ANS) is the part of your central nervous system (CNS) that controls unconscious activities like breathing, heart rate and digestion.

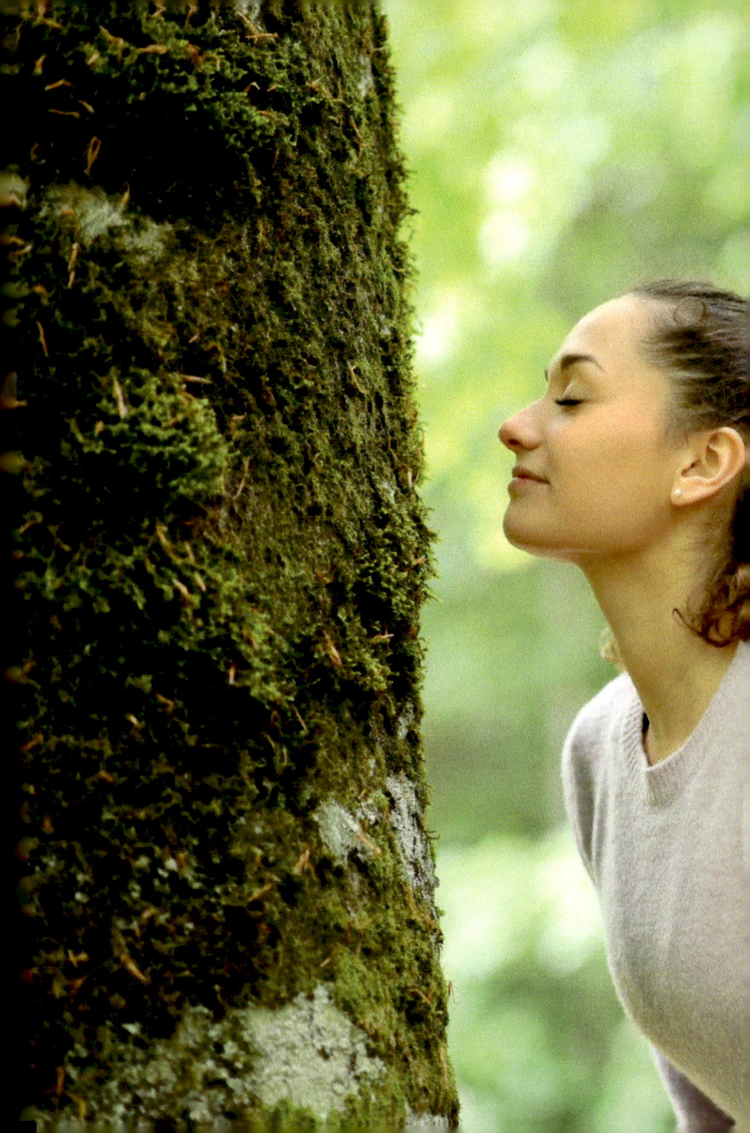

Forest Scents

Pay attention to your sense of smell as you walk through the woods, and when you find a scent, try to follow it. Alternatively pick specific trees, shrubs or flowers to smell, or see if the pine needles from different trees have a different smell when you crush them gently.

Perhaps pick up some leaf litter from the forest floor, scrunch it up and inhale the woodland aroma.

Try inhaling the scent through your nose, and then through your mouth, and see if you can detect subtle differences in how you perceive the scents.

Smell is said to be the sense most closely connect to recall of past people and places. Do any of the smells you find evoke particular memories?

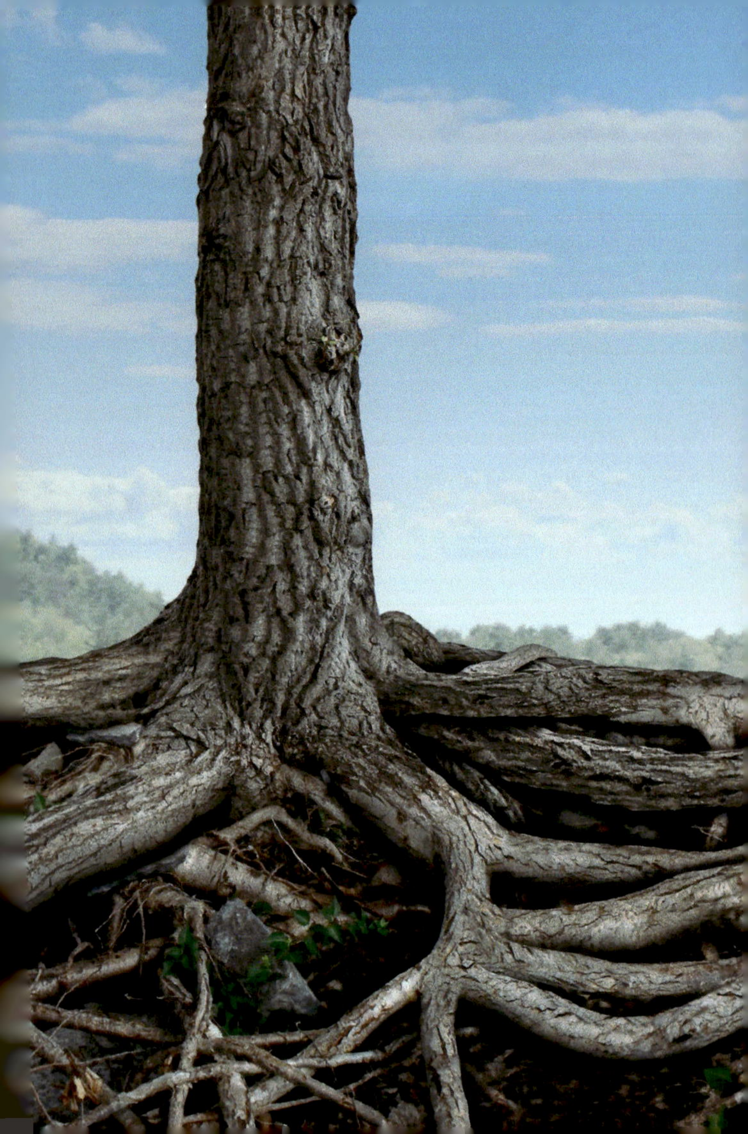

Rooted Like a Tree

Stand and take a look at the trees all around you. Below your feet is an enormous network of tree roots and mycorrhizal fungi invisibly interconnecting the plants and trees that grow above the ground. This network enables the trees to communicate with each other, to swap nutrients and to defend themselves against attacks from herbivores and insects.

Imagine that your feet are becoming rooted into the ground and connecting to this 'Wood-Wide Web'. Allow the trees to help you become aware that you are a part of something much larger than yourself.

How does it feel to be connected to nature in this way?

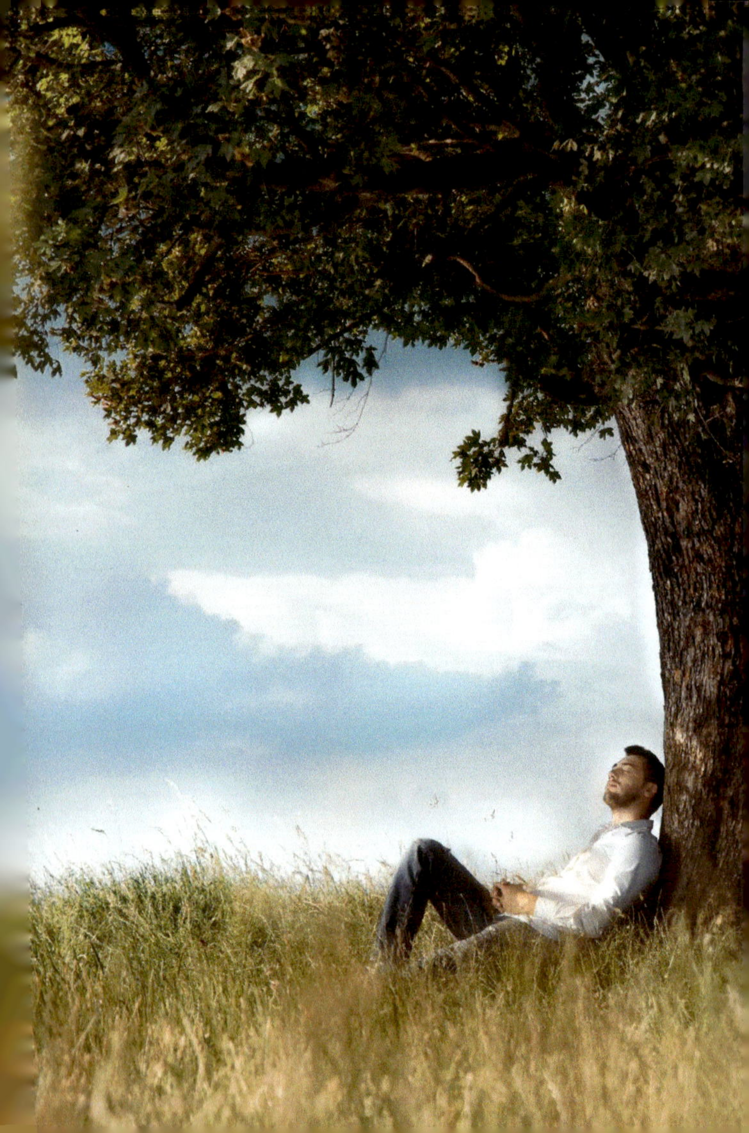

Getting Support From a Tree

Find a tree that draws your attention. Select one that is big enough that you can comfortably lean against it without causing damage, and sit leaning against it for a while.

Notice how it feels to be supported by the tree.

What sensations or emotions do you notice in yourself?

Can you feel the tree moving in the wind? If so, allow yourself to breathe with the tree's gentle movement.

Trees can also provide emotional support. If you have something you want to tell someone, but do not know who to confide in, try telling your inner-most thoughts to your chosen tree.

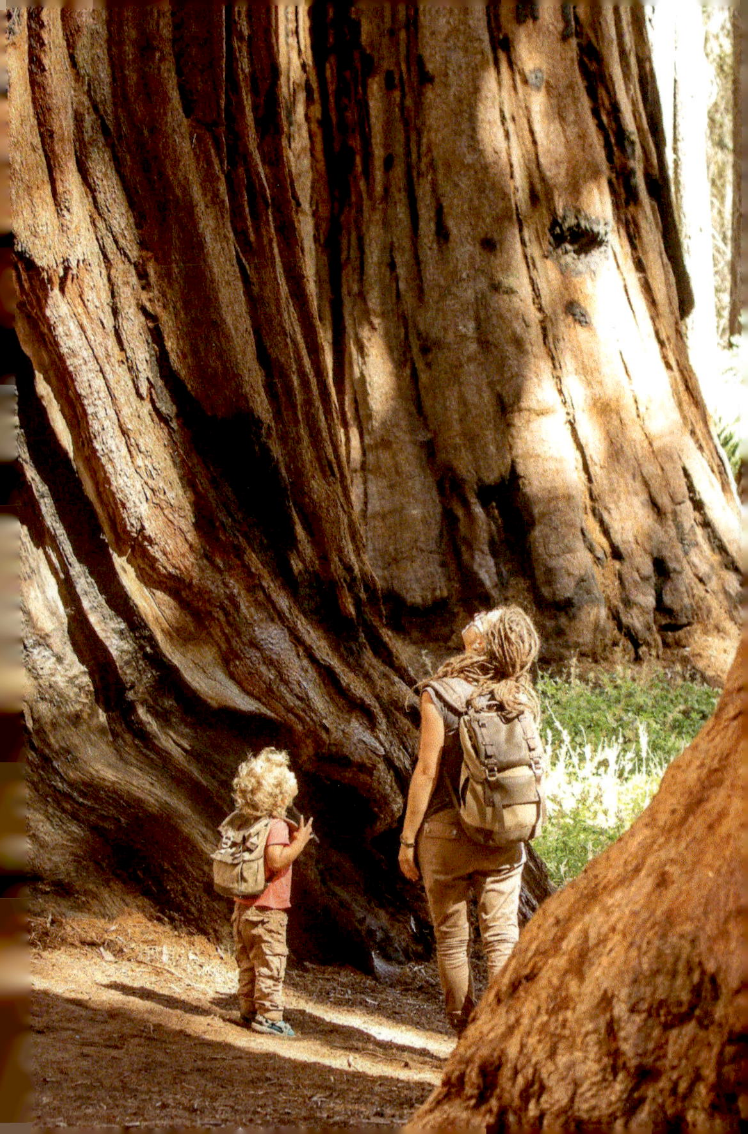

If Trees Could Talk

Approach a tree that you are intrigued by or curious about.

What would it say if it told you its life story?

What do you think that the tree has seen?

What birds have sat in its branches?

Who has sat in its shade?

How has the view it currently has changed as it has grown to the height it is now?

What changes have there been to the landscape since it was a sapling?

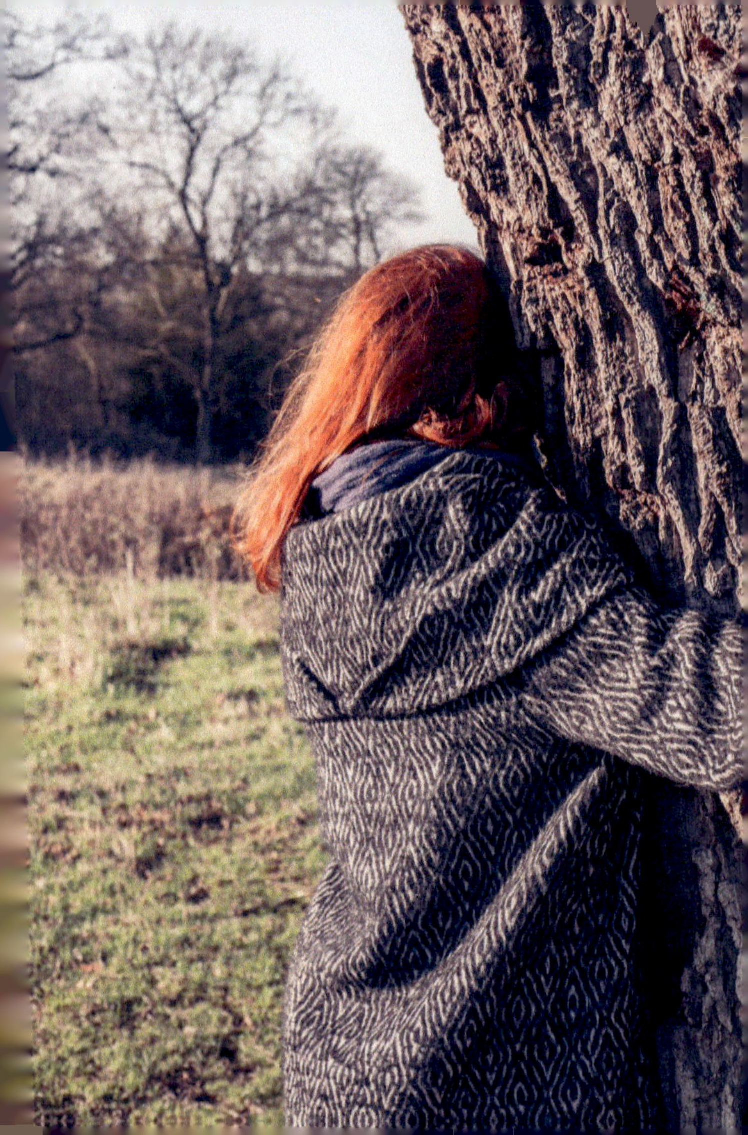

The Texture of Bark

Find a tree with interesting bark that calls out to you.

Stand close to the tree and put your hands gently on the trunk of the tree. Explore the bark with your eyes and your hands.

What do you notice about the texture of the bark?

What colour is it?
Is it rough or smooth?
Is it ridged, furrowed, flaky or cracked?
Is there anything else that you notice living on the bark, either insects, moss or lichen?

Notice how the bark on this tree is different to the bark on other trees.

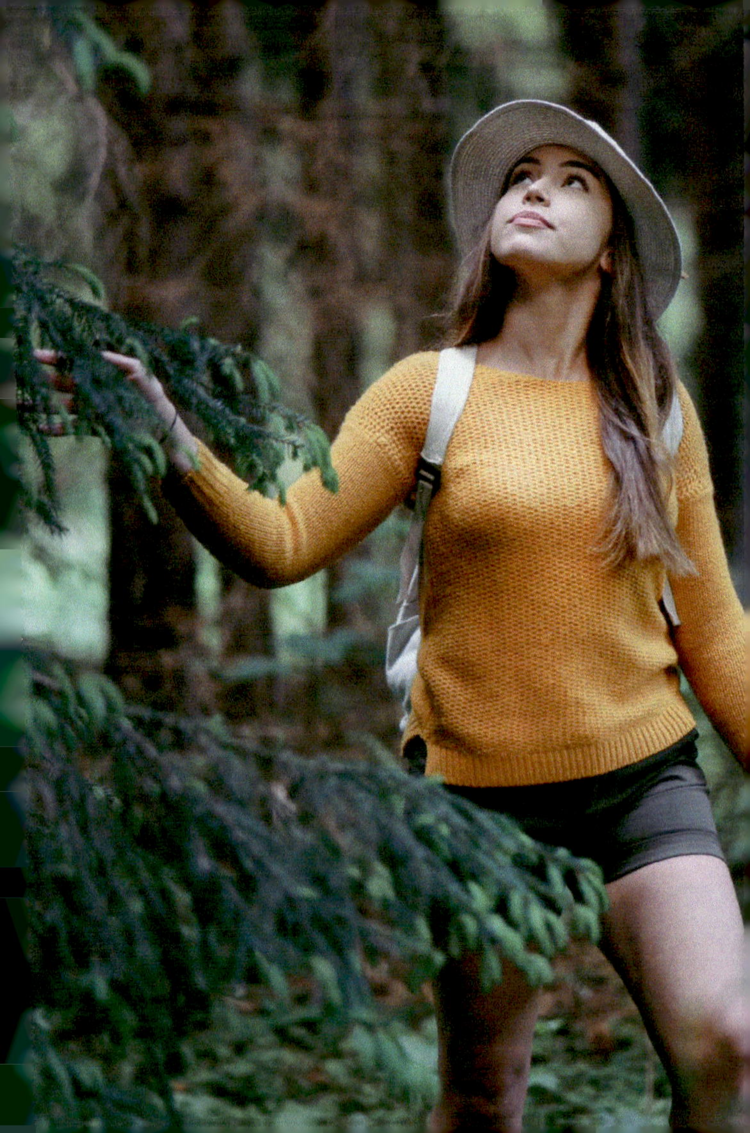

Can't See the Trees for the Wood

Sometimes we just see a wood or forest as made up of lots of trees, without noticing the different trees that there are in there.

Take a walk amongst the trees and look for the differences.

How many different types of trees can you spot? You don't need to know their names, just recognise what makes them different.

Do they have leaves or needles?

What does the bark look like?

What shape are the leaves or needles?

Do they have blossom or berries?

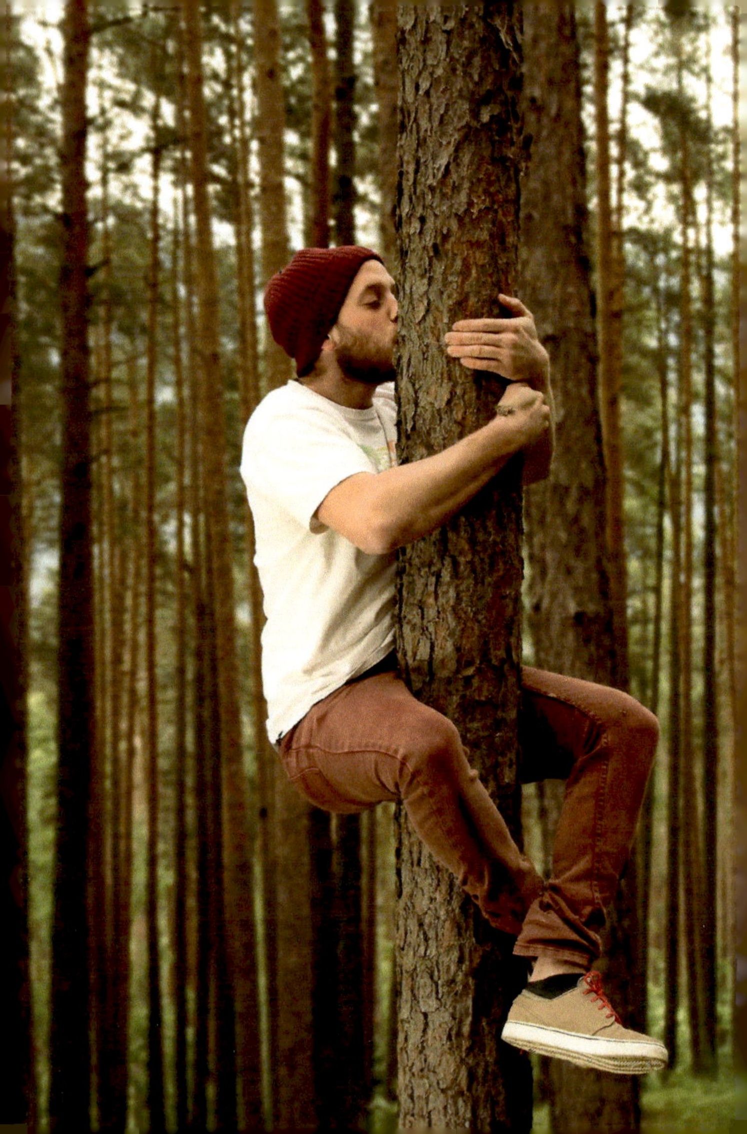

Hug a Tree

Wrap your arms around a tree and give it a hug. Notice its unique characteristics and features.

Do your arms go more than halfway around it?

Rest your forehead or cheek against the tree if you like. Notice how it feels to be in contact with the tree in this way.

If it is sturdy enough, allow it to support your weight. How does it feel to have the tree support you in this way?

Do you feel the tree moving in the wind? Synchronise yourself with this gentle swaying as if dancing with the tree.

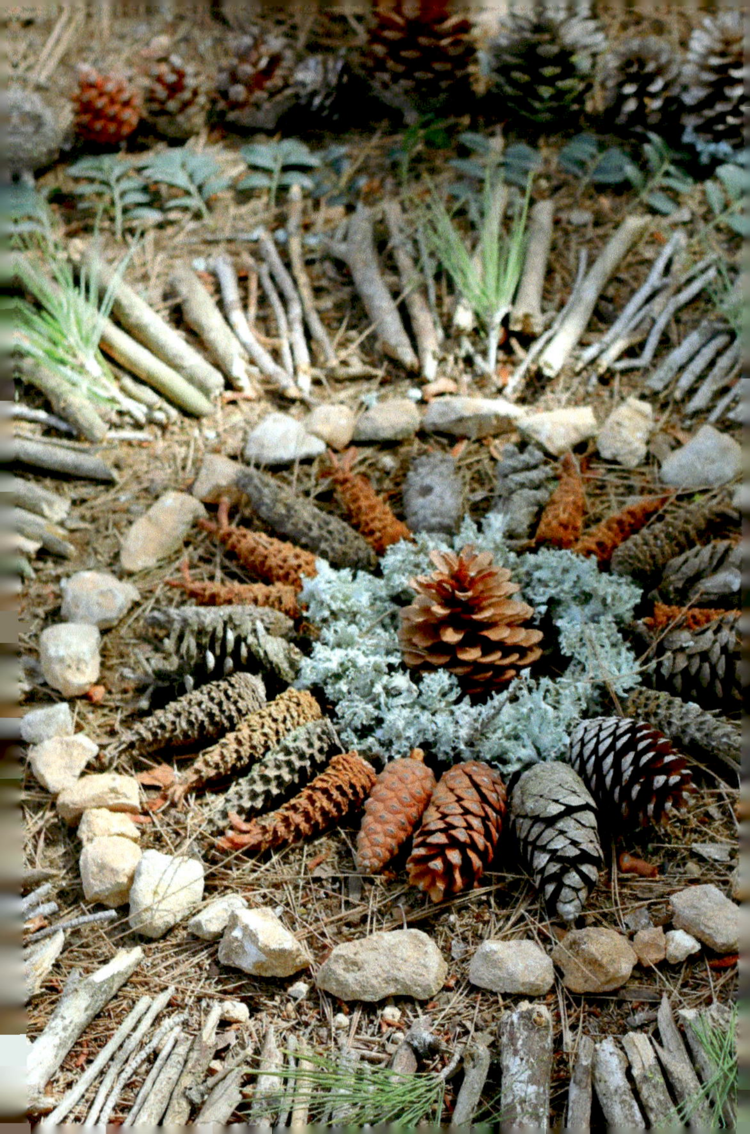

Art That Falls Apart

Sometimes words are inadequate to express our thoughts and feelings. At other times, there is great joy in just creating pieces of art from what nature provides.

Spend some time creating a piece of eco-artwork in nature. You can use stones or pebbles, twigs, leaves, pinecones, seaweed or sea glass, driftwood or anything that you can find that has been created in or shaped by nature, as long as you treat the landscape with respect.

If you like to write poetry, or have a poem related to nature that inspires you or your artwork, feel free to read your poem after completing your piece of eco-art, or write a new poem inspired by it.

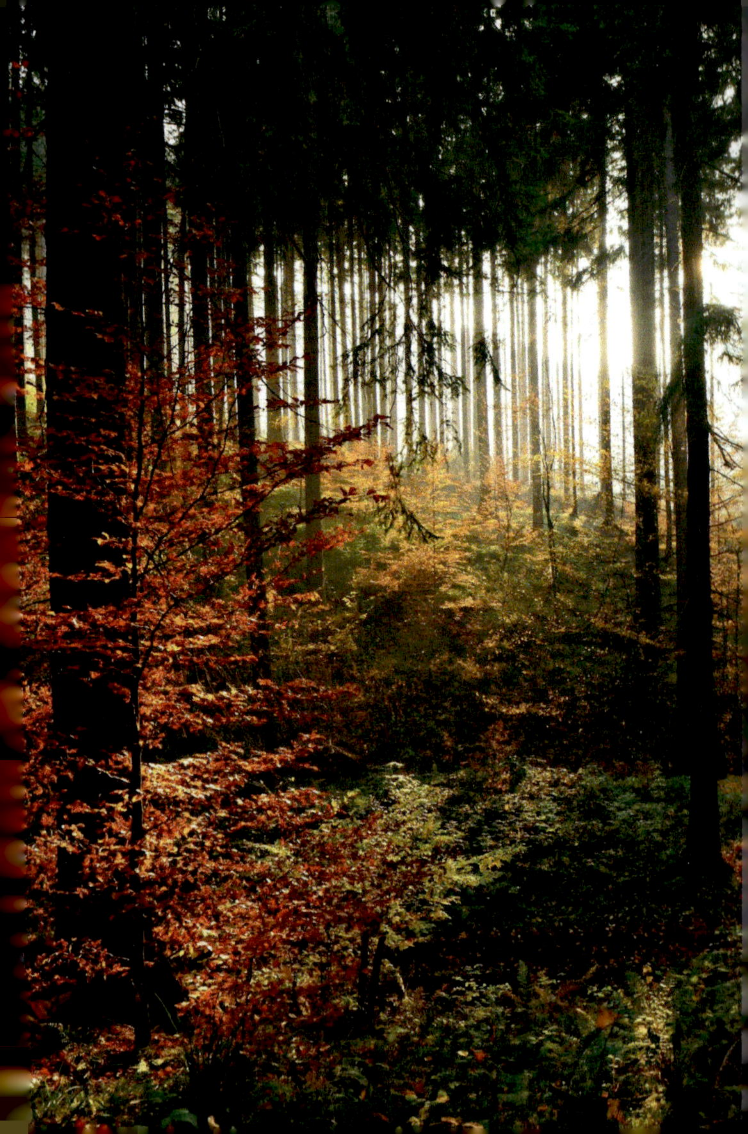

Reciprocity and Gratitude for Trees

When you are amongst the trees in the forest or the woods, pause for a few moments and bring your awareness to the many benefits that they bring. This might be sensory pleasure or from providing shade.

Then take a moment to reflect on the reciprocal (mutually beneficial) relationship that we have with trees. The leaves of trees use sunlight, water and the carbon dioxide they absorb, to make plant sugars, and at the same time they release oxygen. Take a few deep breaths, breathe in the oxygen that you need to live and breathe out the carbon dioxide that the trees need to live.

The appreciation of nature and this reciprocal relationship is a very important aspect of Silvotherapy.

Further Information

This booklet has been written by Hugh Asher, a certified Forest Therapy Practitioner. His vision is to inspire people to improve the health and wellbeing of themselves, of others and of the planet, using nature and nature-connection activities to achieve this.

Hugh is passionate about using the resources found in nature and the natural environment to reduce stress, anxiety and depression; build confidence and self-esteem; and improve mental and emotional health and wellbeing.

If you have any questions, please get in touch - hugh@silvotherapy.co.uk

www.silvotherapy.co.uk

A Small Book of Silvotherapy
© Silvotherapy Limited 2024
www.silvotherapy.co.uk

ISBN 978-1-7385370-0-6

Silvotherapy Publishing